WHY LIZZIE JOHNSON MATTERS TO TEXAS

By Charles Cameron

Published in 2014 by The Rosen Publishing Group, Inc.
29 East 21st Street, New York, NY 10010

First Edition

Developed, written, and produced by Digital Discovery Publishing
Editor: Wendy Scavuzzo
Design & Production: Katherine Berti
Photo research: Crystal Sikkens, Allison Napier
Proofreader: Sarah Cairns

Special thanks to Lynn Peppas

Photo Credits: Austin History Center: 17
Digital Discovery Publishing: 14, 30
The Granger Collection, NYC: 13 (bottom), 19, 20 (bottom), 23, 26, 27, 28
Library of Congress: 7, 11, 14 (top), 16, 22, 25 (top)
National Geographic Stock: Vintage Collection / The Granger Collection, NYC : 1
North Wind Picture Archives: 9, 12, 21
Shutterstock: 5, 6, 13 (top), 20
Southern Methodist University, Central University Libraries, DeGolyer Library: cover, 4
Texas State Preservation Board: 8
University of Texas at San Antonio, Institute of Texas Cultures: 10, 15
Maps by Digital Discovery Publishing

All websites were live and accurate at the time of printing.

Library of Congress Cataloging-in-Publication Data

Cameron, Charles.
Why Lizzie Johnson matters to Texas / by Charles Cameron.
p. cm. – (Texas perspectives)
Includes index.
ISBN 978-1-4777-0908-5 (library binding) – ISBN 978-1-4777-0920-7 (pbk.) – ISBN 978-1-4777-0921-4 (6-pack)
1. Williams, Lizzie Johnson, – 1843-1924 – Juvenile literature. 2. Women ranchers – Texas – Juvenile literature. 3. Ranchers – Texas – Biography – Juvenile literature. I. Title.
F391.W685 C34 2013
976.4–dc23

Manufactured in the United States of America

CPSIA Compliance Information: Batch W13PK: For Further Information contact Rosen Publishing, New York, New York at 1-800-237-9932

CONTENTS

1 SECRET FORTUNE

When Lizzie Johnson died in October 1924, her family was shocked. It was not just that they had lost a beloved member of the family. They were also shocked and surprised to learn that Lizzie had amassed a fortune during her life.

HIDDEN ASSETS

As Lizzie's family gathered to help clear out her belongings after her death, they began to find the traces of a lavish lifestyle they knew nothing about. Lizzie had boxes and trunks filled with beautiful clothes. Some of them were hardly worn. She had diamonds and expensive jewelry hidden in her basement. She had properties and land holdings of more than 65,000 acres (26,305 ha) and $65,000 in the bank. Lizzie was always very private so not even her family members were aware of her wealth.

Elizabeth Johnson was known as "Lizzie" almost all her life.

Lizzie's niece, Willie Shelton, on the surprise of finding hidden treasures throughout Lizzie's house:

> *"I went through her belongings... [and] in an old book case I found hundreds of dollars in five dollar bills. Scattered around the room in various crevices were one hundred dollar bills."*

To many, Lizzie appeared to be a lonely widow who refused to spend any money on herself. In fact, Lizzie Johnson was a woman with great financial talents. She ran many successful businesses in a world dominated by men and grew to become one of Texas's great Cattle Queens.

Texas Perspective

Lizzie Johnson built a fortune during her life. She was worth $245,701 at her death. That would be more than $3 million today!

LIZZIE JOHNSON'S TEXAS

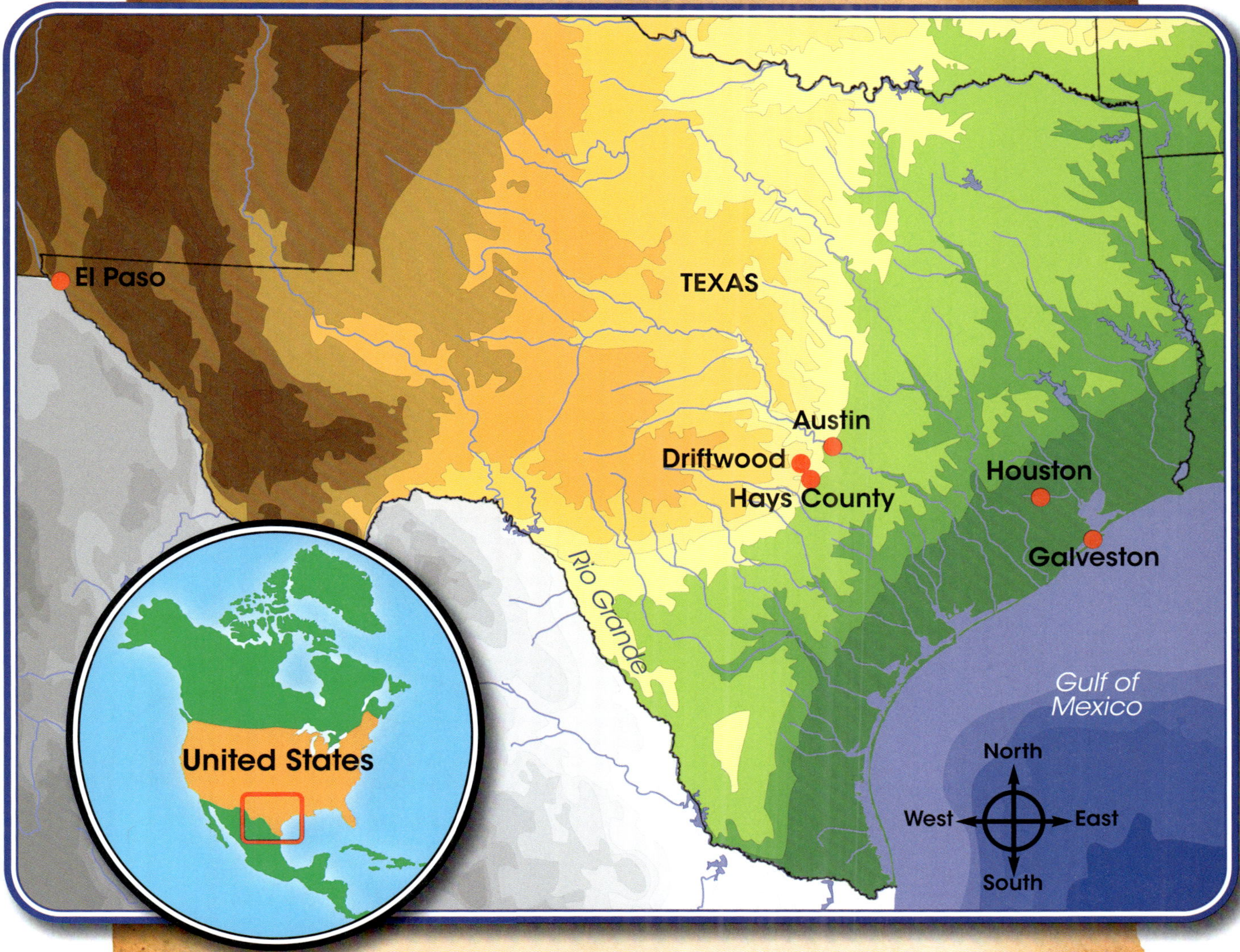

2 EARLY LIFE

Elizabeth "Lizzie" Ellen Johnson was born on May 9, 1840, in Jefferson City, Missouri. Her father, Thomas Jefferson Johnson, was born in Virginia but moved to Missouri as a young man to teach. While he was in Jefferson City he met Catherine Hyde. They were married in 1837 and started a family. Lizzie had an older brother named John and four other brothers and sisters.

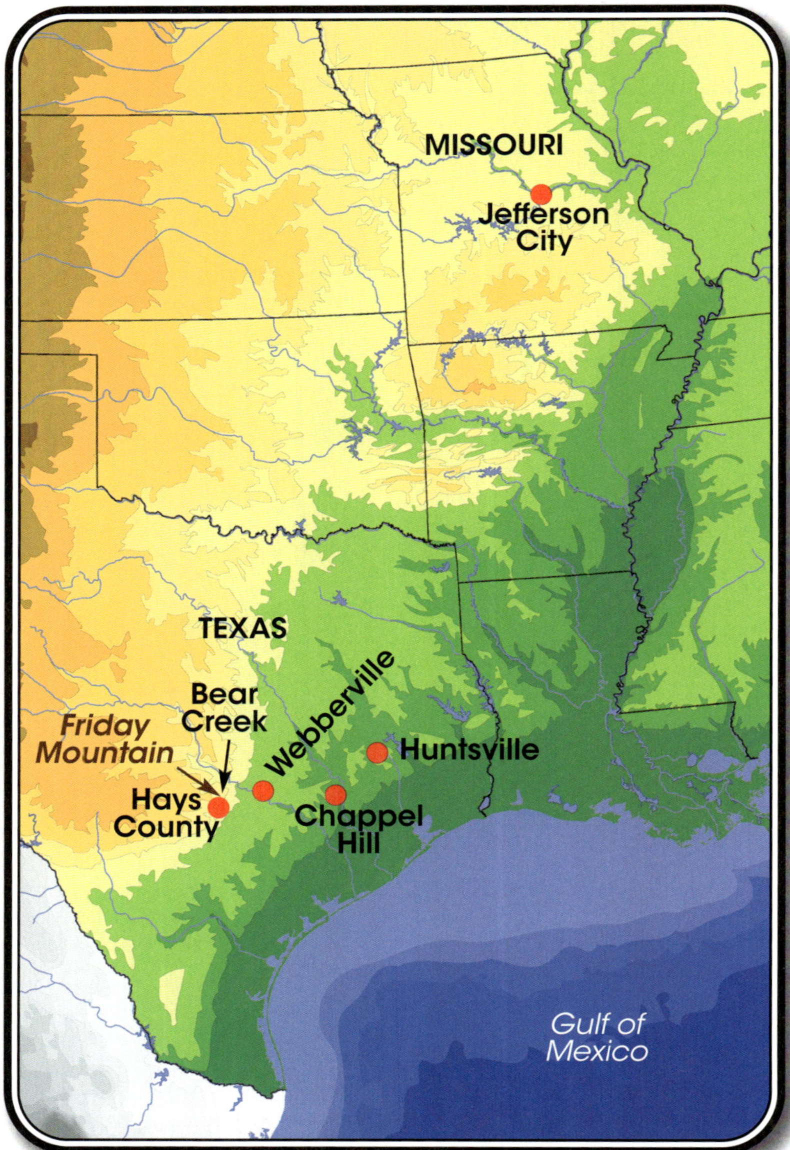

SETTLING IN TEXAS

In 1846, the Johnson family moved to Texas. Lizzie's father dreamed of opening his own school and bringing education to the new state of Texas. In late 1851, Thomas Johnson bought 300 acres (121 ha) of land just south of Austin, Texas. Johnson wanted to build a new school in the countryside, away from the busy city. When the school opened in 1853 it was just for boys. Because so many girls applied, though, it quickly became a school for boys and girls.

Lizzie was six years old when her family moved to Texas. They settled first in Huntsville, but later moved to Bear Creek in Hays County in 1851.

Lizzie's father named his school the Johnson Institute. It began as a simple log cabin but was later expanded to house 200 students by 1868. The school was closed in 1872.

JOHNSON INSTITUTE

The Johnson **Institute** had about 40 students in the beginning. Most of the students were from Texas, but others came from Georgia, Mississippi, and other nearby states. The students lived at the school and were expected to help with chores. Lizzie's father ran the school, and the rest of the family helped out. Lizzie's mother, known as Aunt Katy, taught music, did the cooking and laundry, and **supervised** the girls living at the school.

SCHOOL DAY

Lizzie and her brothers and sisters all attended Johnson Institute. The school day started at 6 a.m. with breakfast. After breakfast, students started their classes. Math, spelling, and grammar were all important parts of the **curriculum**. In 1860, music was added to the list of subjects thanks to the purchase of a piano for the school. Each school term lasted three to four months, and many students began in the first grade and continued on until they had what would be known today as a university **degree**.

EDUCATION IN TEXAS

Texas did not have **public education** when Lizzie and her family arrived in 1846. Texans who could afford it paid to have their children educated in private schools in Texas. Sometimes children of wealthy families from other countries were sent away to live and be educated in the United States. Most children learned from parents or caregivers without ever going to school. Early settlers complained about the lack of public schools when Texas was still a part of Mexico, and it was one of the reasons given for a move toward **independence**. In 1838, when Texas was a republic, President Mirabeau B. Lamar asked for lands to be put aside for public schools. Although tax money was collected for a school system, Texas's first public school did not open until 1873. The Texas Constitution of 1876 brought more changes to the public school system in Texas. Public schools operating in Texas meant that private schools had fewer students attending.

Mirabeau Lamar was the president of the Republic of Texas from 1838 to 1841. He is known as the Father of Texas Education.

TEACHING

When Lizzie turned 16, she began teaching at Johnson Institute. Lizzie taught **bookkeeping**, French, math, music, and spelling. She left the Institute at age 18 to continue her education at Chappell Hill Female College in Washington County. After receiving her diploma, Lizzie returned home to teach again at the Johnson Institute.

Lizzie Johnson was known as a strict teacher, like her father. She once got into trouble for treating a student too harshly.

RELIGION

Religion played an important role in Lizzie's life. She grew up according to strict **Presbyterian** values. The Johnsons read the Bible and prayed together as a family. Lizzie's father would invite different **preachers** to speak at the school on Sundays. Attendance was mandatory for students, and other local citizens would often come, too. When a preacher was not available, Lizzie's father would fill in, telling stories from the Bible to the students. Lizzie remained extremely religious her whole life and recited verses from the Bible at the start of each day.

The Civil War was a war that divided the people of the United States between two sides. Those from the Northern states were called Unionists and fought for the Union. People from the Southern states were called Confederates and fought for the Confederacy. One of the reasons for the war was slavery. The Union wanted to end slavery and keep all the US states together. The Confederacy wanted to break away from the Union and become its own country and protect the right to own slaves. Texas farmers wanted to grow cotton crops, which required a lot of people to work the large farms. The state of Texas left the Union on February 1, 1861, and joined the Confederacy on March 1, 1861. The Civil War began in April 1861 and continued until 1865. At that time, the Confederacy **surrendered** and the Union was **restored**.

JOHN HYDE JOHNSON

Many people in Hays County, where Lizzie lived, supported the Confederacy. Early in the war, Lizzie's brother John joined the 4th Texas Regiment of the Confederate army and went off to fight. John was taken prisoner by the Union army after a battle in 1863 and spent eight months in prisoner-of-war camps. After he was released he was seriously wounded in another battle and lost his ability to speak. John left the army in August 1863. After the war he took a job as a clerk at the Texas Senate. In 1867, rancher William H. Day gave John a job as a bookkeeper. John would often write letters to Lizzie about the cattle business.

William H. Day was a successful rancher. He also tried to convince Lizzie to marry him.

FRANK LESLIE'S ILLUSTRATED NEWSPAPER

No. 1,440.—Vol. LVI.} NEW YORK—FOR THE WEEK ENDING APRIL 28, 1883. {Price, 10 Cents.

▲ Frank Leslie's Illustrated Newspaper *was the largest weekly magazine in the United States in the 1870s. Lizzie published several short stories in the magazine, alongside other famous authors.*

WRITING

Although she was a teacher, Lizzie also had another job. For several years she wrote fiction stories for newspapers and magazines. She used a **pen name** that was different than her own. No one knew she wrote stories until many years later and still no one knows for sure which ones she wrote. The money she earned writing fiction helped her get started in the cattle business.

3 ALL BUSINESS

After the Civil War, Lizzie continued to teach. From 1865 to 1867 she taught in Lockhart, Texas, which was a gathering place for local cattle. Lizzie began to interact with many of the leading cattlemen, and she saw opportunities to make money. She took some of the fees she had earned from her writing and invested $2,500 in a cattle company from Chicago. She sold her investment a few years later for $20,000! She was on her way to becoming very wealthy.

CHANGING TIMES

Things were changing in Lizzie's life. In 1868, Lizzie's father, Thomas, died. The Johnson Institute had 200 students at that time and was doing very well. Lizzie's brother Ben took over running the school. In 1870, the state of Texas introduced a certification system for teachers. Lizzie was granted a "Teacher's Certificate of the First Class" in 1871 and returned to help her family at the Institute. Also that year, Lizzie's brother John died. Finally, in 1872, after 20 years in operation, the Johnson Institute closed and Lizzie went to Austin to teach.

Lizzie was paid very high salaries working as a bookkeeper for local cattlemen. She realized there was much money to be made in cattle.

CATTLE INDUSTRY IN TEXAS

The Spanish brought the first horses to America in the 1500s. They also brought European cattle to the area. They taught the native Mexican people how to raise cattle on ranches, which included the practice of herding cows by workers on horseback. Cow herders, known today as cowboys, were called *vaqueros*, which is the Spanish word for "cowboys." The Spanish settled in Texas in the 1600s, bringing their ranching traditions with them. Before the Civil War the market for Texas cattle was small. Texas ranchers sometimes drove cattle to Louisiana or California to sell. It was cheaper to raise cattle in Texas than in other US states because Texas had the perfect weather conditions and landscape for raising cattle. Once the Civil War broke out, though, all trade with the South was cut off. Many Texas cowboys joined the Confederate army. Texas cattle wandered free for four years and multiplied. When the war ended, hundreds of thousands of cattle could be purchased cheaply in Texas and sold to growing cities in the North for good profit. Texas ranchers **blazed** new trails to move cattle to distant markets where they could make a lot of money.

▲*Texas longhorn cattle are hardy animals that can survive in the harsh Texas terrain.*

▲ *Cow herders, known as vaqueros, used horses to herd cattle in Mexico. This practice was brought to Texas by the Spanish.*

Lizzie bought land and hired cowhands to collect and brand the wild cattle that were roaming freely on the land.

LIZZIE'S BRAND

Lizzie's brush with the cattle industry had stuck with her. She was not satisfied just investing in the cattle business. She wanted to learn everything about it. Using the profits she earned from her first investment, she bought some cattle and land. She also **registered** her own **brand** in 1871. She still continued to teach, but she was quickly learning there was more money to be made in cattle.

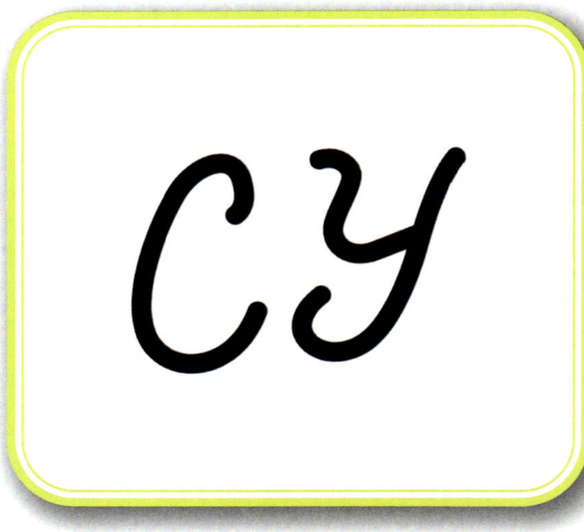

▲ *Lizzie's CY brand was registered in Travis and Hays counties.*

MARRIAGE

Lizzie was a successful, educated, and independent woman. Over the years there had been several men who had wanted to marry her, including rancher William Day. Lizzie turned them all down. She waited until she was 39 years old to get married. This was unusual for the times, but Lizzie always did things her way and on her schedule. When she finally decided to get married, it was to Hezekiah George Williams. Lizzie had met Hezekiah on a trip to visit her brother Ben. Hezekiah was a retired preacher and stock driver. He had been married before, but his wife had died. He had four children. Hezekiah and Lizzie were married in June 1879, and Lizzie dressed very fashionably for the occasion.

Lizzie and Hezekiah Williams were married on June 8, 1879. After she was married, Lizzie became known as Lizzie Johnson Williams.

Lizzie's mother, Catherine, wrote about the wedding:

"[Lizzie] was dressed in a beautiful silk [dress]...and bridal hat...We had a nice cake. Everything went off very nice."

Lizzie and Hezekiah lived in a two-story home in Austin, Texas. Lizzie had purchased the home in 1872. The couple lived upstairs, while Lizzie ran a private school on the main floor.

AUSTIN, TEXAS

The city of Austin, Texas, began on the Colorado River in 1830. It was first known as Waterloo, and very few people lived there. Three years after Texas won its independence and became a republic, President Mirabeau Lamar chose the Waterloo area to develop the country's capital city. A town was planned and it was renamed Austin in 1839. It was named after Stephen F. Austin, who was known as the "father of Texas" because he was the first **empresario** to bring Anglo Americans to live in Texas. The Texas president, Sam Houston, wanted to move Texas's capital to Houston, but the citizens of Austin refused to give up Texas's records and kept them there. After Texas was **annexed** by the United States in 1845, Austin was named the Texas state capital. It remains the capital today.

MARRIAGE BUSINESS

Before Lizzie got married, she made Hezekiah sign a contract stating all her property belonged to her. It also stated that any money she made in the future would be hers alone. This was very unusual at the time and showed Lizzie's independence. She would not rely on anyone and she did not want anyone to rely on her. Hezekiah turned out to be less successful at business than Lizzie, so this was a perfect arrangement. Lizzie's growing fortune would not be at risk if Hezekiah lost money.

BUYING PROPERTY

As another way to increase her wealth, Lizzie started buying property in Austin shortly after her marriage. She bought many Austin buildings over the years. She also owned property in other counties, including Llano, Hays, and Trinity, along with some small ranches. When she died, her **real estate** fortune was valued at $164,339. She made all these purchases without the advice or assistance of anyone else.

One of Lizzie's first real estate purchases was the Brueggerhoff Building in Austin. It was worth $50,000 at the time of her death.

4 CATTLE QUEEN

Lizzie and Hezekiah were both interested in cattle, but they kept their businesses separate. They would arrive at cattle pens together to buy stock but would buy their animals separately. They had a ranch together but hired one foreman to work for each of them separately. Through their entire marriage, Lizzie and Hezekiah operated their cattle businesses in very different ways.

BATTLE OF THE BRANDS

Hezekiah was never as good at business as Lizzie. Although he had been a stock driver before he married Lizzie, he waited until 1881 to register his brand. Lizzie had been in the business for ten years and had benefited from the cattle boom in the 1870s. Hezekiah's timing was not as good, and he entered the business just as the cattle drives were starting to decline. Lizzie proved to be a much better businessperson and had to lend Hezekiah money whenever he would go broke. She always made him pay her back!

Bill Bob, foreman on the Williams ranch, told what it was like working for both Lizzie and Hezekiah:

"Lizzie would instruct [me] to steal Hezekiah's unbranded calves and burn her brand on them... Hezekiah gave [me] the same instructions regarding Lizzie's calves."

BUYING CATTLE

Lizzie was very active in buying and selling her cattle. She would visit stock pens and stand there all day, picking the ones she wanted to buy. Often she would buy and sell in a short period of time, making a good profit. Many times, Hezekiah would be buying at the same time but would lose money in the deal.

Description by an unnamed source of Lizzie Johnson buying cattle:

"She might stand all day long, pointing out the steers she wanted and displaying excellent judgment."

Lizzie Johnson showed great judgment in her cattle selections and business deals.

THE CHISHOLM TRAIL

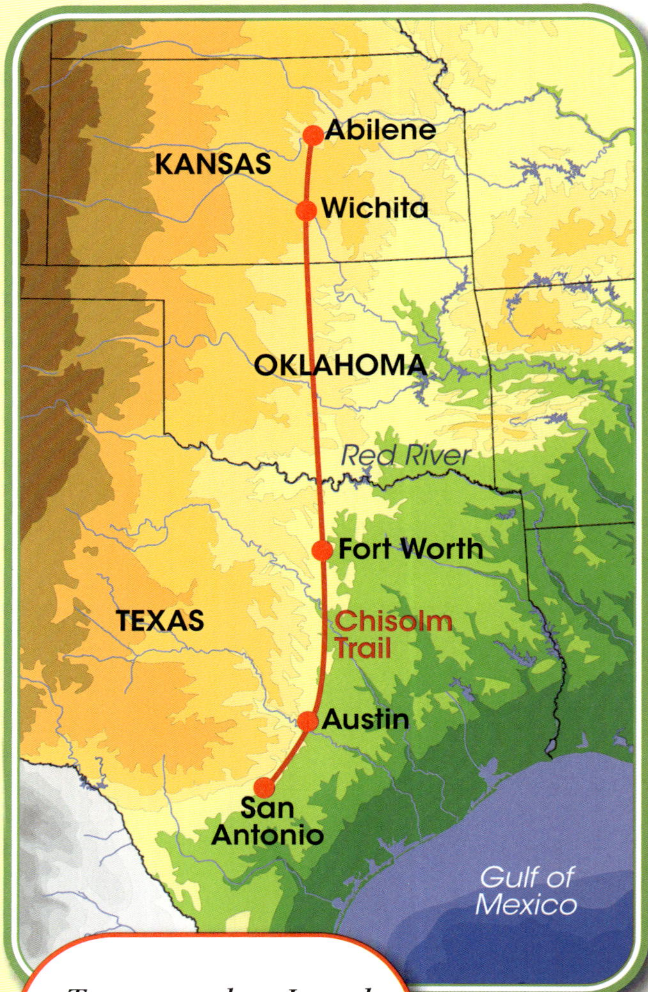

Texas rancher Joseph McCoy got the Kansas Pacific Railway to agree to open a railroad terminal in Abilene, Kansas.

The Chisholm Trail was a trail, or pathway, used by Texas cattle ranchers from 1867 to 1884. At the time Texas ranchers made a lot more money selling their cattle to markets in the northern United States. Cowboys, or vaqueros, drove millions of longhorn cattle on this trail from ranches in Texas to Abilene, Kansas. At Abilene, the cattle were put on trains and shipped to the Northeast.

The trail was named after a trader named Jesse Chisholm. Jesse's father was Scottish and his mother was Cherokee. Jesse first blazed the trail in 1865 to trade goods between Indians and the US Army. Many Texas ranchers, including Lizzie Johnson, soon used the trail to bring their longhorns to market.

▲

Jesse Chisholm also worked as an ***interpreter*** *between Anglo Americans and Indians. He spoke 12 different Indian languages.*

Lizzie would follow behind her herd until they reached Abilene, Kansas.

UP THE TRAIL

Lizzie and Hezekiah went up the Chisholm Trail together with their separate herds at least three times. On the trail, Lizzie was all business. Each morning she would count her cattle to make sure they were all there. She recorded their numbers in a book. She also recorded the hours of the cowhands, so she could pay them at the end of the drive. When the herd reached Abilene, Lizzie sold the cattle, paid the cowhands, and calculated her profits. She was a real cattle woman on these drives at a time when women rarely made the trip.

Mary Taylor Burton, who went up the Chisholm Trail in 1886 with her husband, wrote about the experience:

> ***"...at that time the trip was a very hazardous one...an adventure that tested the courage and endurance of sturdy men, and was considered entirely too dangerous to be undertaken by a woman."***

Texas Perspective

Lizzie is thought to be the first woman to drive her own herd of cattle up the Chisholm Trail.

MEET ME IN ST. LOUIS

Lizzie and Hezekiah would spend falls and winters in St. Louis, Missouri. Lizzie continued to keep the books for cattlemen and write fiction while she was there. She also enjoyed shopping. St. Louis had some of the finest stores in the country, and Lizzie bought new dresses in the latest fashions. Lizzie and Hezekiah stayed in the finest hotels and enjoyed going out for dinner with other cattlemen and their wives. They also spent time traveling to other places around the United States, including Kansas City and New York.

ST. LOUIS, MISSOURI

The city of St. Louis started out as a French fur trading post in 1764. It was the perfect location for traders because the Mississippi and Missouri rivers ran together nearby. The French named it after King Louis IX. St. Louis became a part of the United States when the French sold it to the US in the Louisiana Purchase in 1803. During the 1800s, easy access to railroad and water transportation made St. Louis an important city for business and trade. During the 1800s, thousands of European immigrants to the United States moved there. It expanded to become a center of industry, too.

By 1890, St. Louis was the fourth largest city in the United States.

SHOPPING IN NEW YORK

One place Lizzie liked to visit was New York City. She would conduct business there, but when that was done she would go shopping. New York had many stores selling **elegant** clothes and expensive jewelry. She would buy diamond earrings, pins, and gold rings. Lizzie liked to wear the finest clothes and jewerly when she and Hezekiah went to church or out to dinner parties. In her daily life in Austin, though, she did not dress up at all. She kept all her fancy clothes in boxes or storage trunks in her house.

On one trip to New York City, Lizzie purchased diamonds worth $10,000!

PLANNING FOR THE FUTURE

Things were going well for Lizzie and Hezekiah. In 1896, they purchased a ranch in Hays County, between the towns of Kyle and Driftwood. They began spending much of their time there. Hezekiah also had a dream of building a town on some of their land. However, he began having health problems in 1890. He felt that the best thing for him to do would be to have Lizzie in control of his finances, in case something happened to him. In July 1896, Hezekiah sold all of his stock, land, and cattle to Lizzie.

Hezekiah's statement transferring all his assets to Lizzie on July 30, 1896:

> ***"...I, H.G. Williams, have granted, bargained and sold to L.E. Williams my lawful wife... [all] my land and cattle in Hays County, Texas, or any place whatever, for the sum of Twenty Thousand dollars to me in hand paid by Mrs. L.E. Williams of her separate money to have and to hold forever..."***

NEW CATTLE MARKETS

The demand for Texas cattle in the northern United States began to decline in the mid-1880s. Farmers in Texas and Kansas began putting up fences of barbed wire that made it difficult to drive cattle across the land. As well, Texas fever infected some cattle, and northern buyers looked for cattle from elsewhere, lowering demand further. Finally, as the north recovered from the war, they began to demand better-tasting beef than the longhorn. Texas ranchers began to look for new markets to sell their cattle. One new market was the island of Cuba, located across the Gulf of Mexico.

CATTLE IN CUBA

Christopher Columbus claimed Cuba as a **colony** of Spain in 1492. Spanish settlers brought over the first cattle to Cuba in the early 1500s. Spaniards raised cattle and sold their hides to Europeans. Up until the 1800s, the cattle industry was the main source of income in Cuba. In 1894 there were over two million head of cattle in Cuba. The numbers dropped during times of revolutionary war when Cubans fought against the Spanish for independence. Cuba finally won its independence from Spain in 1898, when the United States won the Spanish-American War. The Treaty of Paris gave the United States control of Cuba. The Americans left in 1902, and Cubans were given control of their own country.

It took about four days to travel from the port of Indianola, Texas (above), to Havana, Cuba. Very few cattle died on the journey.

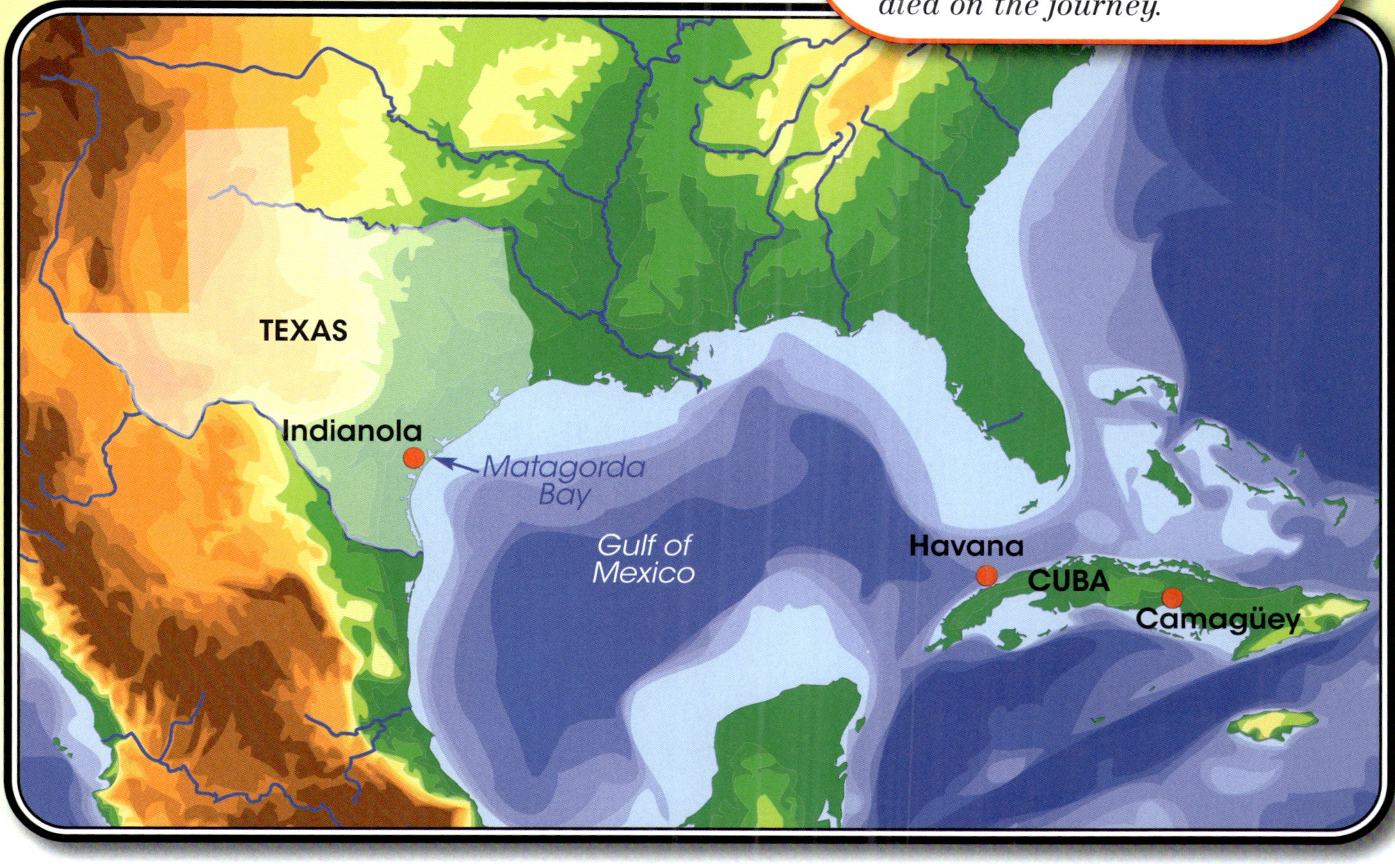

Cattle from Texas would arrive in the port of Havana, Cuba.

JOURNEY TO CUBA

To increase their fortune, Lizzie and Hezekiah decided to move to Cuba and pursue cattle sales there. In September 1904, Lizzie and Hezekiah bought a farm in the Cuban countryside. The farm was near the city of Camagüey. While Cuba was a very good market for Texas cattle, Lizzie and Hezekiah's adventures there were filled with bad luck. One shipment of cattle worth $40,000 was lost. There is also a legend that Hezekiah was kidnapped by bandits and was not released until Lizzie paid $50,000. They returned to Texas in December 1905.

Cuba was an exotic, tropical place. While Lizzie lived there, she acquired a talking parrot, which she brought back to Texas with her.

5 FINAL YEARS

After Lizzie and Hezekiah returned from Cuba, their ranch became the site for a town they called Hays City. Hezekiah spent several years and a lot of money trying to bring the city to life. He planned out streets, hired a foreman to sell lots, installed a windmill, and founded a newspaper. There was even a hotel. Lizzie supported her husband's dream, and together they built a church in the town, which also served as a school. It was not to be, though. Bad luck turned potential residents away and the city was never completed.

HEALTH CONCERNS

Hezekiah's health had never been very good. It got worse as he got older. Lizzie would often take Hezekiah to Hot Springs, Arkansas, and other spas in the United States to help restore his health. Eventually, they went to El Paso, Texas, for warmer temperatures and more sunshine.

HOT SPRINGS

A hot spring is a body of water on Earth's surface that is much warmer in temperature than its surrounding area. The water in hot springs is heated below Earth's surface. Water trickles slowly through Earth until it reaches miles (km) below and is heated by a layer of rock heated by Earth's magma. The hot water then rushes upward to the surface in natural springs. One American city famous for its hot springs is Hot Springs, Arkansas.

◀ *Hot Springs, Arkansas, was a popular health resort in the 1800s.*

DEATH OF HEZEKIAH

Although the climate in El Paso was meant to help his health, Hezekiah died on July 26, 1914. Lizzie went to the undertaker and purchased an expensive coffin. She brought his body back to Oakwood Cemetery in Austin and buried him there. Lizzie had a granite tombstone put up to mark the final resting spot of her beloved husband.

Lizzie wrote on the bill for Hezekiah's $600 coffin:

"I loved this old buzzard this much."

El Paso, Texas, has a hot climate with little humidity. The sun shines on average 302 days per year. El Paso is nicknamed "the Sun City."

WIDOW

After Hezekiah died, Lizzie maintained her investments and business activities. She sold off the ranch in 1920. The hotel in Hays City was taken down so that the wood could be used to build new structures. Lizzie made money with each transaction. Lizzie moved into a single room in the Brueggerhoff Building, which she continued to own. She would make frequent trips to the bank, where she was held in high regard because of her excellent credit. She also went to the post office every day.

Lizzie did not take good care of herself as she got older. She wore old black clothes, and a black hood or bonnet. Her room was dark and cold. She refused to burn more than one piece of firewood at a time. She was eating only a bowl of vegetable soup with bread every day, for which she paid ten cents. She had a glass of orange juice brought to her every day for five cents and complained when the merchant tried to raise it to seven cents. She began to get a reputation for being a miser and a person with no friends.

Lizzie's grandnephew Emmett Shelton on Lizzie's refusal to spend money on herself:

"...a restaurant owner... would send dinners up to her every day. She thought he was the nicest man because she thought the dinners were free. She never knew that we paid for them."

DEATH

By 1924, Lizzie was too frail to live on her own. She needed more care. Lizzie was not close with much of her family but moved in with her niece Willie Shelton. She lived in Willie's house on West Live Oak Street, in Austin, until she died on October 9, 1924. She is buried in Oakwood Cemetery next to Hezekiah.

6 LIZZIE'S LEGACY

Lizzie Johnson was ahead of her time. She was a woman who succeeded in the Texas cattle business at a time when it was dominated by men. She built a fortune based on her own skills, intelligence, and determination. She refused to allow anyone to tell her what she should do or how she should do it. As a result, she was often on the better end of her financial deals and investments.

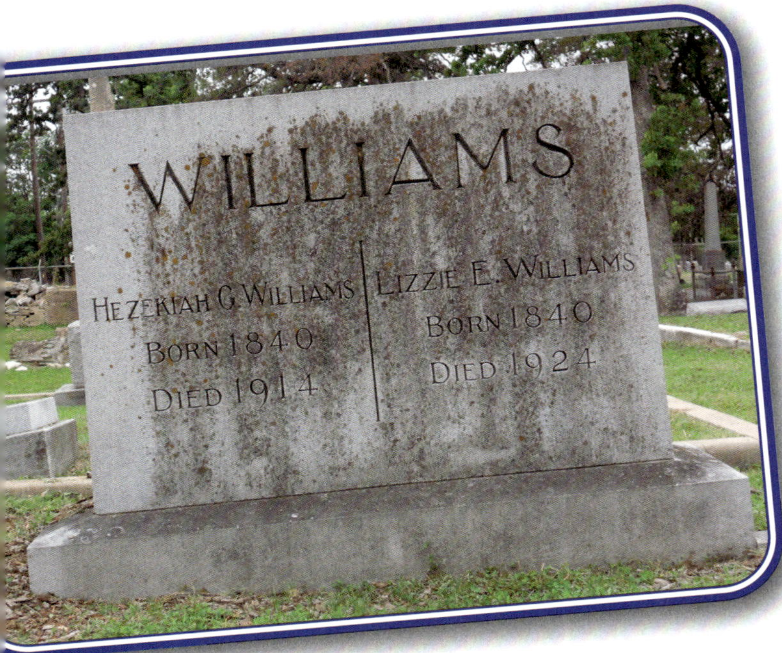

Lizzie's niece Willie wrote about her aunt's legacy in 1947:

> *"There can be no denying that she was not only a gallant frontier Texas woman in the cattle trade but also a pioneer among women in the field of finance."*

◀ *Lizzie and Hezekiah are buried side by side in Oakwood Cemetery in Austin, Texas.*

LEARNING MORE

BOOKS

Schwartz, Heather E. *Lizzie Johnson: Texan Cowgirl.* Huntington Beach, CA: Teacher Created Materials, 2012.

WEBSITES

Chisholm Trail Heritage Center
www.onthechisholmtrail.com

Chisholm Trail Heritage Museum
www.chisholmtrailmuseum.org

Women in Texas History
www.womenintexashistory.org

TIMELINE

Texas	Lizzie Johnson

1837 Thomas Jefferson Johnson and Catherine Hyde marry

Updated pages on ftp: May 9, 1840 Elizabeth "Lizzie" Johnson born in Jefferson City, Missouri

1846 The Johnson family moves to Texas

1851 Thomas Johnson buys land in Hays County, Texas

1853 Johnson Institute opens

1856 Lizzie starts teaching at Johnson Institute

1858 Lizzie attends Chappell Hill Female College and receives diploma

1861 On March 1, Texas joins the Confederate States of America. Civil War begins on April 12

1863 John Hyde Johnson captured in Civil War battle

1865 Civil War ends

1865 Lizzie teaches at Lockhart until 1867

1868 Thomas Jefferson Johnson dies

1870 Lizzie teaches at Parson's Female Seminary

1871 Lizzie receives teaching certificate; registers cattle brand; brother John dies

1872 Johnson Institute closes

1879 Lizzie marries Hezekiah G. Williams; travels up the Chisholm Trail with her herd of cattle

1896 Hezekiah signs over all his property to Lizzie

1904 Lizzie and Hezekiah buy a farm in Cuba and live there until 1905

1914 Hezekiah Williams dies in El Paso, Texas

October 9, 1924 Lizzie Johnson Williams dies in Austin, Texas

GLOSSARY

annex (a-neks) To take over or add to.
blaze (BLAYZ) To mark out or clear a new trail.
brand (BRAND) A mark with a certain design burned on to an animal's hide by a hot iron pole.
bookkeeping (BOOK-kee-ping) The job of recording business transactions.
colony (KAH-luh-nee) A new place where people move that is still ruled by the leaders of the country from which they came.
curriculum (kuh-RIK-yuh-lum) The course of study in a school.
degree (dih-GREE) A title given to a person who has finished a course of study.
elegant (EH-lih-gint) Showing good taste.
empresario (em-pruh-SEHR-ee-oh) A general manager with broad powers and responsibilities.
independence (in-dih-PEN-dents) Freedom from the control or support of other people.
institute (IN-stih-toot) An organization that aids a certain cause or group.
interpreter (in-TER-prih-ter) Someone who helps people who speak different languages talk to each other.
pen name (PEHN NAYM) A name an author uses that is different from his or her own name.
preacher (PREECH-er) A person whose job it is to give talks about God.
Presbyterian (prez-bih-TEER-ee-un) Of or relating to a branch of the Christian church.
public education (PUH-blik eh-jeh-KAY-shun) Schools run by the government that are available to all children.
real estate (REEL es-TAYT) The business of selling land and houses.
register (REH-jih-ster) To record in an official book.
restore (rih-STOR) To put back, to return to an earlier state.
supervise (SOO-per-vyz) To manage and direct work or workers.
surrender (suh-REN-der) To give up.

INDEX